On the Origin of
DIGNITY

Its Creation and Enhancement

Walter W. Tunstall, Ph.D.

Archway Publishing books may be ordered
through booksellers or by contacting:

Archway Publishing
1663 Liberty Drive
Bloomington, IN 47403
www.archwaypublishing.com
1 (888) 242-5904

ISBN: 978-1-4808-5174-0 (sc)
ISBN: 978-1-4808-5173-3 (hc)
ISBN: 978-1-4808-5175-7 (e)

Library of Congress Control Number: 2017954135

Print information available on the last page.

Archway Publishing rev. date: 09/11/2017

To the memory of

Elizabeth Powers Tunstall:
One of nature's noblewomen

Contents

Preface ix

Introduction xi

Chapter 1 Evolving Meanings and Usage............................1

    The Latin *Dignitas* 2

    Thomas Aquinas 2

    Giovanni Pico della Mirandola 3

    Immanuel Kant 3

    Religious and Theological Accounts 4

    Confucius 5

    Dignity and Human Rights..6

    Dignity and Bioethics..7

    Dignity and Business...8

Chapter 2 Dignity's Relationship to Language and Current Usage 9

Chapter 3 The Reflexive Nature of Self-Conception 13

Chapter 4 Dignity as a Psychological Process 17

    Dignity Is a Social Process 19

    A Common Area of Confusion.....................................22

    Recent Research on Self-Esteem and Self-Concept.......23

    Dignity as a Reciprocal Interactive Process...................25

Validation and Valuation Are Different Processes 28

Dignity as a Personal Sense of Worth..............................31

Differences between Dignity and Related Ideas............38

    Dignity and Reward and Punishment.......................38

    Dignity and Power 39

    Dignity and Interactionist Theory............................41

Measurement..42

The Components of Dignity 46

    Dignity and Behavior 46

    Dignity and Suicide 48

Chapter 5   Research Findings Thus Far............................49

    Gender...50

    Race 51

    Age...51

    Clinical Group..55

    Self-Esteem...58

Chapter 6   Intersubjective Validation 59

    Desideratum 60

    What Difference Does All This Make? 61

References 71

Acknowledgments..83

Index 85

Preface

S ometimes, life gets in the way. I began this book approximately thirty years ago, following the completion of my doctoral dissertation, titled "Dignity: A Psychological Construct," and its publication in *Dissertation Abstracts International*. At the time, it was my intention to produce a book that would introduce my research on the origin and development of dignity. The book was intended to be primarily of interest to other psychologists and scholars. Then the life part happened.

Following a stint at St. Leo University, where I taught fourteen undergraduate psychology courses, I spent the next twenty-eight years working as a psychologist in public agencies, providing services to persons with chronic disabilities. During the first decade of my professional career, I was mostly involved with persons with developmental disabilities who lived in residential centers. The remaining years of my career were spent as a staff psychologist in a large psychiatric hospital, where I provided services to a diverse mix of people who had been diagnosed with major mental illnesses, traumatic brain injuries, or developmental disabilities.

The book that you have before you is in numerous ways substantially different from the one I had originally intended to write. Indeed, I discarded the chapters I began in 1985. They did not speak to the wider audience that I now would like to address. In addition to substantially altering the tone of my earlier writing, which had originally been intended for specialists and scholars, this book addresses a more general audience. In preparation for undertaking the completion of this offering, I have become reacquainted with much of what has been written about the topic of dignity during the intervening years.

Additionally, it was necessary to reimmerse myself in what has been published in the field of psychology, regarding the self and the development of the self-concept. Another way this book differs from its predecessor is the greater extent to which applications of dignity theory are discussed as it applies to various domains of everyday experience.

Introduction

For many of us, dignity is an idea we readily embrace, in addition to other of our most cherished beliefs, like love, justice, and freedom. But exactly what we mean when we think about dignity is never called into question. We simply accept that dignity exists, and that in all likelihood we have it. But where does our dignity come from? How do we get it?

The answer to each of these questions may not be, upon reflection, as readily evident as is frequently assumed, nor as clearly defensible as is frequently believed. Indeed, some writers (Macklin, 2003; Pinker, 2008) have in recent years argued that dignity doesn't exist at all or that it is at best redundant and adds nothing new to our understanding of the human condition. While it is my opinion that dignity exists, I will argue that its origin and, to a lesser extent, its place in contemporary discourse differs from many of the beliefs currently held. The account I will offer is shaped primarily through my vantage point as a social psychologist, not through the more familiar lens of philosophy, religion, politics, or legal thought. Thus, the perspective presented here is essentially a psychological one. It places the origin of dignity squarely within the experience of each individual person, or more precisely within the dependent and emergent intersubjective experience of individuals in interaction with one another. As such, dignity is experienced within a social psychological process, and as I will argue, in the absence of the process, it does not exist.

While such a perspective may seem divergent from more familiar accounts of dignity, the account provided here is, I believe, foundational to many long-held beliefs regarding dignity, and it is, as I hope to show, compatible with most contemporary uses to which dignity is put.

In recent years, dignity (or the frequently encountered term "human dignity") has become a subject increasingly found in public discourse, as well as in specific domains such as philosophy, politics, theology, religion, law, medicine, nursing, and bioethics. A review of the growing and rather extensive literature related to dignity finds that the term means different things to different people. Most current beliefs about dignity's origin can be organized into two general perspectives: One view of dignity sees it as social in origin because it frequently refers to a person's place within a hierarchical social order; in other words, a person's social rank. The other perspective is frequently more transcendent in origin and draws upon philosophical, religious, and theological belief to explain where dignity comes from and why it is important.

In this book, it is not my intention to provide a detailed or nuanced account of the numerous contributions made by earlier writers regarding the origin and meanings of dignity. Fine recent accounts can be found, for example, in McCrudden (2013), Rosen (2012), Kateb (2011), and Waldron (2015). Instead, I will offer a brief and general snapshot of some of the more influential and frequently cited writers and their thinking regarding dignity in order to provide a historical and contextual reference point for my own thinking on the topic. This will show how my work is similar to and different from existing accounts of dignity and how a psychological perspective can provide a more incisive and individually meaningful account of a person's sense of dignity. Additionally, I hope to show how this psychological perspective may help to clarify some of the long-standing and seemingly incompatible beliefs that pertain to the origin of dignity.

One of the principal reasons for presenting the following ideas is to address, and hopefully bring some clarity to, an aspect of dignity discourse that has troubled me from my earliest involvement with the topic: the problem of reification. For readers unfamiliar with this idea, it refers to treating an abstract idea as if it were a concrete thing. Such is the case, it seems to me, with dignity and, more particularly, the problem with human dignity as it is currently understood.

Few would deny that dignity is a lovely idea (or perhaps even a great idea). Indeed, dignity may be well on its way to becoming one of the more cherished and influential ideas in this period of our cultural evolution; that is, if the increasing occurrence with which references to dignity are seen as an indication of its growing importance (see again McCrudden, 2013; Rosen, 2012; Kateb, 2011; Waldron, 2015; and Kass, 2004). However, merely because an idea is lovely, or because we like it, doesn't entitle us to claim that this thing actually exists, no matter how devoutly we may wish it to be so. Such usage, in dignity's case, frequently seems to be an instance of the classic confusion in thought of *is* and *ought*. The eighteenth-century Scottish philosopher David Hume, in his *Treatise on Human Nature*, is credited with the idea that you can't deduce *ought* from *is*. That is to say, merely because something is doesn't allow you to conclude that it ought to exist.

My concern is that the inverse of Hume's maxim is also too frequently seen. That is, persons who strongly believe that a certain thing *ought* to exist conveniently, but unfortunately and mistakenly, come to believe that it does indeed exist or *is*. In a case such as dignity, we may like the idea of dignity so much that we come to believe that if it doesn't quite exist, it certainly ought to exist, and that people ought to be treated as if they possessed dignity. In instances such as this, our belief in the *oughtness* of dignity becomes transformed into the *isness* of dignity, and miraculously what ought to be is, and as a result, people now have dignity. As time passes, the isness of dignity is adopted by believers who unquestioningly accept its existence.

More substantively, an additional source of human dignity's susceptibility to question arises from the explanations regarding its origin. Many accounts allege that dignity, rather than being a quality naturally possessed by humans, is instead derived from some other thing. The other thing is presumably sufficiently valued such that by our association with, or our identification with, the valued thing, we acquire dignity. Such attempts to provide a rationale for human dignity are in essence saying that dignity is not a quality humans possess, but we may acquire it by association with something more important, something more valued than we ourselves are.

Such accounts of dignity's origin may rely on theological arguments, purporting a relationship with a deity; social arguments, affording placement within a status hierarchy; individual accomplishment, conferring excellence upon an individual; or exhibiting appropriate social behavior as the basis for inferring that a person possesses dignity. Arguably, one of the most influential accounts within the Western cultural tradition regarding the origin of dignity was provided by the German philosopher Immanuel Kant. Kant essentially said that because we are human beings, we have dignity or intrinsic worth. Admittedly, this is a lovely idea and likely one that has warmed the hearts of despairing souls for centuries, but dignity, according to Kant, is nevertheless derived from elsewhere. It is dependent upon some other thing. Another way to express this is to say that human dignity is attributed to a person based upon some other valued attribute. A bit more will be said about Kant a little later.

In the first chapter that follows, priority will be given to a brief tracing of the most often cited ideas regarding dignity within the Western cultural tradition (with a brief nod to Eastern thought, as well). While I acknowledge that the section will likely be seen as unrepresentative of the breadth of dignity's history, it is my intention to provide merely a broad orientation to the evolution of beliefs about dignity, in an effort to show how we have come to hold our current beliefs about the concept. Further, this orientation will serve to show how my own thoughts on the subject of dignity are dissimilar from as well as continuous with those that have come before.

Chapter Two will review the meanings dignity has acquired during its venerable course over the centuries, revealing those aspects of the term that have remained mostly unchanged and those that have augmented its meaning. My intent in including this section is to show how my use of the term is an extension of dignity's long tradition of usage.

Chapter Three will present contributions by major American writers on the reflexive and social origin of our self-concepts.

Chapter Four will describe in detail my ideas on the origin and development of dignity, as they were originally presented in my doctoral dissertation at Virginia Commonwealth University.

Chapter Five will present selected findings that resulted from the development and testing of a self-report inventory that measures a person's sense of dignity, and which may be of interest to specialists and nonspecialists.

In Chapter Six I will describe dignity as a social psychological process. This perspective affords a unifying lens that integrates aspects of Eastern and Western tradition regarding the origin of dignity, while casting its emergence and development irretrievably within the phenomenal ontology of the individual person.

A brief discussion of how the view of dignity offered here may influence existing social practices and institutions will follow.

1

Evolving Meanings and Usage

The following constitutes a brief synopsis of the more frequently referenced and historically significant writers who have shaped our modern understanding of dignity.

The modern term that we know today as "dignity" has a venerable past, extending backward for thousands of years. It has not, however, always been used to mean what we mean when we use the term today. Indeed, there is not universal agreement regarding exactly what dignity means when it is referenced today. An ongoing dialogue among discussants representing law, politics, philosophy, religion, and theology continues to seek a consensus on what is intended when the idea of dignity is invoked. Like other elements of human culture language evolves over time to reflect human needs and the uses to which a word is put. The ongoing dialogue regarding the meaning of dignity is expressive of its evolving place in the lives of people everywhere, and it is to the ongoing evolution of this dialogue that the voice of this endeavor is lent.

The Latin *Dignitas*

An early and often cited example to which the term dignity has been put is found in Cicero's *De Officiis* (*On Duties*). He uses *dignitas* as a status term to refer to how the best men in a well-ordered society should live. His use of the term seems to refer to "honor," or an honored place in society, and it also refers to the respect due to individuals who occupy such a position. Cicero further suggests that the dignity of human beings arises from our superiority to other living creatures. By including all human beings as a class, he broadens the domain within which a human can be said to have dignity from the merely individual to something more universal.

Thomas Aquinas

In his Commentary on the Sentences, Catholic writer Thomas Aquinas offered this definition of dignity: "Dignity signifies something's goodness on account of itself." That is, a particular thing has an intrinsic worth because of the position it occupies in a divine order created by God and revealed to humankind through Scripture. Aquinas's view of dignity's origin shares with Cicero's a common assumption that its origin derives from our place in a hierarchy—albeit one hierarchy is divine and the other profane.

Giovanni Pico della Mirandola

During the Renaissance, another noted example of dignity emerged, with a somewhat different meaning. It equated dignity with worth. This variation in meaning is found in a fifteenth-century work by Giovanni Pico della Mirandola, *Oration on the Dignity of Man,* in which he affirms that it is the human capacity for self-creation that distinguishes us from the rest of creation. Mirandola argues that we choose our own destinies by our natural capacity to shape ourselves within a range of possibilities that are not available to other living creatures. This, he opines, is the basis for humanity's special place and worth. Mirandola's analysis implies that it is by our ability to engage in self-creation that we have dignity.

Immanuel Kant

During the eighteenth century, the German philosopher Immanuel Kant provided an account of dignity that has attained considerable historical significance. In his *Foundations of the Metaphysics of Morals,* Kant asserted that human beings have dignity because we, each of us, have unconditional and incomparable value—that is, intrinsic worth. He apparently saw this value arising, in part, from the human capacity to be self-directing: "Autonomy is therefore the ground of the dignity of human nature." As a consequence, Kant believed that human beings should always be treated as ends in themselves and never as means to another end. He additionally affirmed that humans have dignity because human beings, and human beings alone, are the bearers of morality. As such, humans have dignity so long as they have morality. In Kant's account, dignity is something that all human beings possess by virtue of being human, and it is not something specific to a particular individual or an individual's social position or status.

Religious and Theological Accounts

Religion and theology have made substantial contributions to our current discourse on the origin of human worth or dignity. Theologians in particular are increasingly engaged in describing how human dignity relates to religion. As David P. Gushee in *Understanding Human Dignity* notes, "The Hebrew Bible and New Testament have for thousands of years expressed the God-given sacredness of each human being."

Gushee offers the following thoughts:

> To say that each human life (or human life, as such) is sacred, is to claim that God has consecrated each and every human being—without exception and in all circumstances—as a unique, incalculably precious being of elevated status and dignity. Through God's revelation in Scripture and Incarnation in Jesus Christ, God has declared and demonstrated the sacred worth of human beings and will hold all human beings accountable for responding appropriately. Such a response

begins by adopting a posture of reverence and by accepting responsibility for the sacred gift that is a human life. It includes offering due respect and care to each human being that we encounter. It extends to an obligation to protect human life from wanton destruction, desecration, or the violation of human rights. A full embrace of the sacredness of human life leads to a full-hearted commitment to foster human flourishing.

Confucius

Within Confucian teaching, dignity is seen as the worth that individuals acquire by behaving appropriately in their relationships with others. The relationships are established in terms of two interdependent virtues: *Jen*, which refers to our relatedness to one another and the requirement that in order to be fully human, we must take other individuals into account and treat them appropriately. The second virtue, *Li*, refers to the rules guiding proper behavior. Becoming fully human and having dignity are seen as two elements comprising the same idea. Accordingly, we acquire our human relatedness, or *Jen*, through our interactions with others, and we learn the rules of *Li* from our family and society, which instill within us our humanity. As such, neither our dignity nor our humanity is innate. Instead, it is acquired through our interactions with others (Chang, 1980).

Dignity and Human Rights

In recent years, the domain of human rights has become one in which dignity has increasingly gained prominence, both in discourse as well as in numerous political and legal documents. Increasingly, human dignity is affirmed to be the basis for specific human rights and for the laws that uphold them. There are several examples of well-known documents in which the importance of dignity is prominently established, like the preamble of the 1948 United Nations *Universal Declaration of Human Rights*. The declaration refers to "recognition of the inherent dignity and of the equal and inalienable rights of all members of the human family." Perhaps somewhat surprising to readers unfamiliar with this area of political history is that the pairing of the ideas of dignity and human rights was not frequently seen prior to 1948.

Human dignity is also given a prominent place in UNESCO's *Universal Declaration on Bioethics and Human Rights*. This declaration is in part a response to the development of new biotechnologies that some believe undermine or threaten values many feel are important to our humanity.

An additional and notable example of the centrality dignity has taken on within the human rights arena in recent decades is seen in the inclusion, by some countries, of dignity as a constitutional right. In such instances, dignity is introduced in an effort to assure that political, social, civil, and economic liberties are legally upheld. Both Germany and Israel have embraced dignity as a constitutional right of its citizens.

Dignity and Bioethics

Bioethics is an area in which dignity has garnered significant attention. Ongoing developments in biotechnologies and neuroscience have introduced what many consider to be potentially significant threats to fundamental values regarded as central to what it means to be a human being.

In Article 2(d) of the UNESCO *Universal Declaration on Bioethics and Human Rights* (2005) the following affirmation of purpose is presented:

> Recognize the importance of freedom of scientific research and the benefits derived from scientific and technological developments, while stressing the need for such research and developments to occur within the framework of ethical principles set out in this Declaration and to respect human dignity, human rights and fundamental freedoms.

There have been numerous developments in medicine, nanotechnology, and neurotechnology: DNA sequencing, stem cell research, cloning, abortion, in vitro fertilization, euthanasia, and genetic engineering that have raised concerns regarding intrusions into human nature and violations of human dignity. As a consequence, the call for regulatory oversight has been substantial.

Dignity and Business

Growing attention is being given among businesses, particularly within international negotiations, to the importance of conducting transactions that take into account the dignity of the individuals involved in the transactions, and a recognition that substantially different beliefs regarding the origins of dignity may exist within different cultural orientations. For example, business partners with a Western worldview who see dignity as an innate and inalienable characteristic arising from rational capacity and transcendent origin may find it beneficial to be aware that other potential business associates with an Eastern worldview have a different conception of how dignity originates: behaving honorably with good intentions and promoting harmony and reciprocity (Koehn and Leung, 2008).

2

Dignity's Relationship to Language and Current Usage

I nasmuch as dignity is a term that has been in use for several thousand years, the question some will likely ask of this writer is: why tinker with the meaning of dignity? Why not leave well enough alone? The paragraphs that follow will provide a brief account of the various meanings dignity has taken on, as well as call attention to an enduring and consistent core of meanings that have been maintained throughout its long history. This summary, which some may find somewhat pedantic and otherwise tedious, is, nevertheless, intended to allow readers to more meaningfully and critically engage with the idea of dignity as it will be introduced later. I further hope to show how the shared meanings associated with dignity, both historical and contemporary, are expressive of an underlying, and what I believe to be, universal psychological experience. It is this fundamental psychological phenomenon that will be addressed later in my explanation of the origin of dignity as it arises and is experienced in each individual person to a greater or lesser degree.

A survey of major English language dictionaries reveals a fairly consistent core of meanings or designates for dignity. *Webster's Unabridged Dictionary* provides the following entries: "the quality or state of being honored or esteemed, degree of esteem, honor, worth, worthiness, merit, rank or title of honor, gravity, and poise." *The Random House Unabridged Dictionary* provides the following entries: "bearing, conduct or speech indicative of self-respect or appreciation of the formality or gravity of an occasion, nobility or elevation of character, worthiness, degree of excellence, elevated rank, office, and station." *The Oxford English Dictionary* records the first noted use of dignity in the English language as 1225. The dictionary further indicates that dignity was then used and has continued to be used to mean: "the quality of being worthy or honorable, noble and excellent." The meaning for the French equivalent of dignity, *digne*, parallels its English counterpart via designations of high worth or desert, worth, honorable, and excellent.

Practically all of the long standing meanings associated with dignity, as well as its contemporary social and cultural expressions, appear compatible with the conceptual framework provided by dignity as an individual's psychological experience. Moreover, these meanings can be divided into three general categories of experience and designation, which may in turn help to clarify dignity's place as a psychological process within conventional discourse.

The first category of meanings specifically equates dignity with worth. Indeed, there appear to be no instances, within the romance language tradition, where dignity does not mean at least worth, or a state of worthiness. Such a condition establishes a strong tradition and precedent for the equivalence of dignity and worth; an association that will find further expression in my description of dignity as a person's sense of self-worth in the paragraphs to follow.

A second category of meaning includes a number of lexical entries that are valuetive in nature: excellence, honor, esteem, elevation and relative standing, or rank. These terms are expressive of dignity's link to the valuation process. Valuation and validation are distinct but related processes in the creation of dignity, and each provides an essential function in its creation. Their roles will be explored in greater detail in the description of the theory that will follow.

A third category of designation: conduct or speech indicative of formality, gravity or occasion, poise, station, and office appears in general to fit Marcel's (1963) "decorative" conception of dignity. It is in this decorative element, Marcel maintains, "We more or less confuse with the display of pomp that usually accompanies power. It is considered advisable, for example, to surround judicial power with appearances and conditions likely to command respect or, if one prefers, to put a certain distance between men entrusted with high duties and ordinary people" (p. 128).

While it is readily acknowledged that there are numerous uses of the term dignity that will not strictly overlap with the use of the term as it is given here, this offering will, nevertheless, focus on the psychological and behavioral aspects of the human experience of self-worth or dignity, not the metaphorical and allegorical references that appear in other uses of the term.

In view of the foregoing considerations, several significant precedents offer themselves for undertaking the use of dignity to refer to an individual's personal experience of self-worth. First, there is considerable historical precedent for the equivalence of dignity and worth. Additionally, numerous instances of a similar association between dignity and worth can be found within contemporary language and daily usage. Both of these conditions suggest a broad recognition and acceptance of the equivalence of the idea of dignity and worth within our everyday experience.

3

The Reflexive Nature of Self-Conception

The following paragraphs provide an overview of prominent contributions made by writers regarding the interdependent and reflexive nature of our beliefs about ourselves: our self-concept.

Numerous writers in the area of interpersonal dynamics have focused on the phenomenal and situated nature of interactive experience (Berger and Luckman, 1966; Cooley, 1902; James, 1890, 1892; Mead, 1934, 1956; Sartre, 1948). From this perspective, the objective world is often seen as absurd. The things, the events, and the relationships that occur in the world have no meaning apart from those that we choose to give them. Meaning from this view is an interpretation, a mental construction that we impose on the circumstances in which we find ourselves. The meanings that accrue for certain things and events are generally seen to be social in origin because it is through ongoing interactions with others that we acquire a basis for constructing shared meanings for things in the world. From this vantage point, "the locus of interpersonal relations is in the individual's mind where all experience is organized, interpreted, forgotten, and remembered" (Van Mannen, 1979, 19).

An aspect of interactive experience that has received attention from numerous writers is the self. William James (1890), who is generally regarded as the first self-psychologist, divided the self into three parts: the material self, the spiritual self, and the social self. He appears to have located this social sense of self in the minds of other people. According to James, the social self is based on the acknowledgment that an individual receives from other people: "A man has as many social selves as there are individuals who recognize him and carry an image of him in their minds" (p. 294).

Charles H. Cooley (1902), a sociologist, and the next major figure to deal with the idea of self, took a more sociological perspective than James. Cooley was concerned with the aspect of the self referred to by James as the "social me." It was in his "looking glass" conception of the self that Cooley argued for your conception of yourself as determined by the perception of other people's reaction to you. A sense of self, therefore, is not possible without an awareness of other people's reactions to yourself.

Following Cooley, George H. Mead (1934, 1956) likewise saw the self as a social phenomenon, a product of interaction in which individuals experienced themselves as reflected in the behavior or the reactions of other persons. Mead, like those self-theorists who preceded him, saw the origin of the self in the I-Me distinction: the process by which an individual becomes an object to him or herself (Wells and Marwell, 1976).

According to Stanley Coopersmith (1967), another writer interested in the self, the concept of self as an object is a complex one: "It is formed out of the diverse experiences and different levels and types of competence one possesses for dealing with the environment" (Coopersmith, 1967, p. 21). The self from this point of view is regarded as multidimensional, and the various dimensions represent the range of individual experience (Dobson et al., 1979; Fleming and Watts, 1980; Marsh and Smith, 1982). Two widely noted dimensions of the self as object are self-esteem, the personal satisfaction with our role or quality of performance, and self-concept, the perception(s) we have of ourselves in terms of personal attributes and the various roles we play (Beane and Lipka, 1980). More recently, numerous researchers (for example, Blackhart et al., 2009; Liu and Baumeister, 2016; Forsyth et al., 2007) have investigated the relationship between self-esteem and other variables such as narcissism and social ostracism.

Dignity is an additional dimension that reflexively contributes to our relatively stable, socially derived self-concept, but which has received relatively little attention within the self-conception or interpersonal literature. Indeed, most accounts of dignity, as we have seen, come from disciplines other than psychology. In most previous accounts, dignity has been approached as an ethical or legal construct rather than a psychological one. Current formulations tend to place dignity in a normative role, focusing on proscriptive or prescriptive expectations within interpersonal/social interactions.

4

Dignity as a Psychological Process

A review of the existing literature on dignity reveals it to be conceptually rich and, at the same time, diffuse and amorphous. The meanings represented by dignity comprise a multiplex of beliefs, shades of nuance, emotion, and tradition, which have led to multiple and sometimes fervently held viewpoints. In short, apart from the dignity/worth synonymy previously noted, there appears to be little in the way of a coherent conceptual framework that unifies the meanings of dignity. A tradition of usage appears to be the primary unifying factor.

Dignity as it will be presented here does not provide a wholly unifying perspective through which the entire and evolving kaleidoscope of dignity's uses and meanings may be understood. That is not the primary desire nor the intent of this writer. Instead, grounded in a phenomenal approach to social cognition, this book provides a psychosocial explanation from which the origin and development of an individual's personal sense of worth may be understood.

To regard dignity as an intersubjective psychological process may occasion some initial disequilibrium, as this different way of thinking about personal worth is assimilated into existing patterns of thought. However, the potential benefits that accompany such a change outweigh the rather negligible drawbacks associated with the revision. In the past, given dignity's primary status as a reified ethical construct, it has frequently served as a polemical device for mounting ethical arguments in cases where belief in individual or human worth has been a consideration. As a psychological process, dignity becomes a living, dynamic expression of the human condition, not something that one necessarily has, but something that can be created, nurtured, developed, and sustained. Given, moreover, that dignity from this perspective is an interpersonal creation based on experience, it becomes possible to consider the possibility of systematically modifying individual dignity through individual experience. The potential for reducing unhappiness through the enhancement of a sense of personal worth should offset any general discomfort that may be associated with dignity's transition from an ethical imperative to a malleable and assessable component of an individual's psychological makeup

To state the obvious, if individuals have dignity, they know it; it is self-evident to them. It's less obvious to say that it would be preferable if they did not have to rely upon an act of faith or the ingestion of a doctrine, no matter how lovely or alluring, in order to believe in their personal worth or dignity. Alternatively, the perspective offered here describes how our phenomenological ontology (our experienced first-person point of view or structuring of our awareness) becomes personal dignity and is grounded in the intersubjective experience that takes place during social interaction.

Dignity Is a Social Process

Dignity as formulated here provides a recently developed and integrative framework within which the various historical references and social uses to which dignity has been put may be understood. Each of the three previously mentioned general categories of usage (dignity as worth, dignity's link to valuation, and dignity as decorum) share a common characteristic: Each category is behaviorally anchored. Each individual term expresses a common characteristic that inheres in overt behavior that traditionally has been associated with dignity. The commonalities found in the various behaviors associated with dignity are socially shared and overt expressions of the underlying psychological experiences of worth, and they reflect the structural and dynamic elements of the individual psychological processes of the person involved.

As the term is generally used in everyday speech, dignity is not seen when behavior is mindless or reckless. Nor are persons who behave in vulgar ways usually thought to be dignified. Dignity takes place (is created) when we engage with someone else in a process of mutual and interdependent validation of each other's beliefs, feelings, or behavior. Validation refers, in this instance, to the reciprocal ratification, conformation, or justification of each individual's emotions, beliefs,

or behavior. Imagine, for example, two individuals meeting and interacting for the first time. When validation takes
place, a certain amount of psychological distance is involved.
This distance is suggested by Gabriel Marcel's (1963) decorative conception of dignity. The distance, or more appropriately, reservation, is a necessary and integral aspect of the
validation process. To be validated by another person typically requires us to be mindful of the other person's possible
reactions to us, and we usually present ourselves to them in
a manner that we anticipate will lead to positive valuation.
Valuation is then followed by validation or nonvalidation.

As suggested here, valuation and validation are distinct
processes. The reserve frequently associated with so-called
dignified behavior is an inherent element and a behavioral
consequence expressive of the recognition that valuation as
well as validation (or invalidation) are at play. The cognitive
and behavioral reserve that follows from the requisite mind-
fulness of the role we play in another person's validation, and
the potential consequences their reaction may have for us, is
expressive of the mutually interdependent phenomenology of
dignity. In established relationships where mutual valuation
and validation have been repeatedly practiced, reserve may
be unnecessary, and spontaneity may dominate.

A further illustration of how the commonalities found in
the socially shared meanings of dignity reveal the underlying
psychological process of worth that has given rise to them
can be seen in the group of definitions referred to earlier
as the valuetive category. In the "dignity as value" category

are found such terms as relative standing, excellence, and elevation. The validation process is linked to the valuation process such that failure on the part of an individual (A) to value another individual (B) renders B's validation of A of little or no account. In other words, dignity has not occurred. The valuetive dimension represented by such terms as "excellence," "elevation," and "relative standing" acknowledges the importance a source of validation may have for someone. Conversely, at the opposite end of the valuetive dimension, terms such as "worthless," "inferior," and "low-grade" are expressive of low valuation, and they determine, as before, the extent to which validation may take place.

Thus, the link between behavior as it is expressed through the socially shared categories of meaning (dignity as worth, dignity as value, and dignity as decorum) and the intersubjective psychological process of validation (as it is experienced as a personal sense of worth) makes dignity an appropriate term to represent these observed consistencies in behavior, as well as an individual's internal psychological experience.

The use of dignity to designate the psychological experience of worth shares an extensive precedent within psychology for taking terms widely used in ordinary daily speech and redefining them in specific and theoretically useful ways to bring conceptual clarity and technical specificity to the field. Examples of how psychology has taken commonly used terms and given them technical meanings quite distinct from their everyday use include "reactance," "torque," and "discrimination," to name a few. The differences between the psychological experience of dignity and its general use to mean personal worth describe clearly what has been implicit in the use of the term for millennia. The current offering simply articulates what many individuals have consciously grasped (or may have but dimly felt).

Some will likely argue that there are drawbacks associated with the use of the term dignity as it is being defined here. Their objections, for the most part, likely arise from ancillary or secondary uses associated with the term dignity as it is popularly used and which are mostly at variance with dignity as it is being defined here. An example of such incompatibility is seen in the phrase "the dignity of the mountain."

A Common Area of Confusion

It has only been since the work of James Diggory (1966) and other social psychologists that the particular aspect of our self-concept and self-structure known as self-esteem has become widely studied. Inevitably, the different methods used by individual investigators in their assessment of self-esteem have reflected the investigator's unique conceptual formulation. These differences have been reviewed and extended by Burns (1979); Crandall (1973); Wells and Marwell (1976); Wylie (1961, 1979); Showers, Ditzfeld, and Zeigler-Hill (2014); and Baumeister et al. (2008).

Writers in the area of self-conception, in general, and self-esteem, in particular, have frequently used terms such as "self-concept," "self-regard," "self-esteem," "self-worth," "self-respect," "self-evaluation," and "self-estimation" interchangeably, or at least with little apparent regard for conceptual or practical differences between the terms. This tendency has led to terms of self-conception that are in general inconsistent or vague, or which have their distinctions substantially blurred (Bean and Lipka, 1980; Brownfain, 1952; Coopersmith, 1967; Fitts, 1965; Gergen, 1971; Gordon, 1968; Korman, 1968; Marsh, Relich, and Smith, 1983; Rosenberg, 1979; Shavelson, Hubner, and Stanton & Stanton", 1976; Shibutani, 1961; Symonds, 1951; Taylor, 1955; Webb, 1955).

In many instances, dignity, or the psychological experience of personal worth, has been conflated with definitions of self-esteem and self-evaluation. Efforts have been made to define self-conception dimensions both in theory and research, although slight attention has specifically focused on dignity. Researchers such as Marsh, Parker, and Smith (1982); Marsh, Relich, and Smith (1983); Marsh, Smith, and Barnes (1982); and Shavelson et al. (1976) have provided strong empirical support for a multidimensional model of self-conceptualization, a model compatible with the increased differentiation of terminology and structure implicit in the present formulation of dignity. To date, however, little effort appears to have been made to distinguish between dignity and esteem, or dignity and other dimensions of self-conception.

Recent Research on Self-Esteem and Self-Concept

Examples of more recent attempts to further clarify dimensions of the self-structure include efforts by Harter, Waters, and Whitesell (1998); Marshall, Parker, Ciarrochi, and Heaven (2014); and Gadin and Hammarstrom (2003), who focused on the role social validation plays in self-worth. Other writers have used longitudinal studies to focus on the relationship between age and self-worth (Erol and Orth, 2011; Robins and Trzesniewski, 2005) or self-worth and external contingencies (Burwell, 2006; Wouters et al., 2013). These efforts, nevertheless, continue to conflate worth with esteem.

Given dignity's historical status as a social and an ethical imperative, its more recent emergence as a political and legal construct, and its conceptual and terminological conflation within the area of self-conception, little precedent exists for thinking of dignity as a psychological dimension or process. To regard an individual's sense of personal worth in this manner, however, is helpful for several reasons. First, to regard dignity as the psychological experience of personal worth provides a means for describing a process through which an individual's sense of worth comes into existence; that is to say, where dignity comes from. It avoids the previously noted confusion of is and ought, and it avoids the need to attribute dignity to someone based on peripherals such as doctrine, dogma, social status, or esteemed behavior.

Second, it provides a means for explaining why and how individuals can be differentiated on the amount of dignity they possess, why some individuals feel they have considerable worth, and why other individuals feel they have little worth. Third, dignity as psychological process describes a behaviorally anchored interpersonal and ontological nexus from which individual persons engaged in interaction with one another literally create, or co-create, one another's, each other's, being in the world: their worth, their dignity.

Dignity as a Reciprocal Interactive Process

The position taken here regarding the conditions from which dignity/worth originate are generally in agreement with the position taken by symbolic interactionists: Human existence is given but itself has no meaning. From this viewpoint, meaning becomes possible in relational situations in which influence and consequence follow from interaction. Meaning in this view is an emergent phenomenon. It comes into being as the process of interaction takes place. Meaning, therefore, is social in origin (Stern, 1975).

Some might argue that humans have worth, and hence dignity, because we are the originators of meaning. This is, of course, an important consideration, but it is not the principal aspect of the interactive process that will be focused on here. The genesis of worth/dignity is intimately tied to the interactive process. Humans are not seen, in this formulation, as having worth because of something else: because of a relationship with God, because of our ability to think, or even because we are human. Worth is not seen as a derivative function of some other thing, condition, or circumstance. Instead, worth is seen as a constantly renewable and emergent phenomenon. Worth takes place, emerges, from within the interdependent and intersubjective phenomenology of one human being interacting with another human being, as validation or invalidation. The process always takes place

whether we are aware of it or not, or whether we want it to
or not. Worth is, thus, an interactive and emergent creation,
a co-creation, and as such does not exist apart from interpersonal experience.

The experience of human worth emerges, as noted,
through a process of reciprocal validation that occurs when
one human being interacts with another human being. That
is, human life has meaning and worth as each individual in
interaction with another human being becomes a source of
validation (justification, ratification, confirmation) or nonvalidation of the other person's experience (thoughts, feelings,
behavior).

Worth is manifest through the act of objectifying or
bringing into the experienced phenomenal world the perceptions (beliefs and emotions) of each individual engaged in
the interaction. Through the process of validation, individual
phenomenology, our awareness of the contents of our consciousness, is taken from the personal, the subjective, and the
imaginary and is given an existence outside the differentiated
consciousness associated with the self. Through the process
of validation, consciousness achieves authenticity; it becomes
real.

When thoughts, emotions, or behavior are validated by
another individual, the validation affirms that a contribution has been made to all that is, that something had been
added, that something legitimate has been created in the situated moment when interaction occurred, and phenomenal

existence has been augmented. The interactive creation has been granted legitimacy by the validation of the persons involved.

Invalidation implies an individual's offering has not made a contribution to all that is. Accordingly, the offering is essentially unworthy of authenticity; it is invalid, and it is not to have existence nor admittance into the phenomenal and experienced world. In other words, it will not be acknowledged as real. In cases such as this, an individual's efforts have resulted in the creation of a *no thing*. To have created a no thing is to have created nothing. To have intended to create something, but instead to have had one's creation invalidated, affirms that one's efforts are pointless, useless, and perhaps, by inference, the individual person, the creator's, existence likewise has less of a place in all that is. Many of us are likely familiar with the statement "I'm not going to dignify that by saying anything" when we encounter something exceptionally offensive or absurd.

Failure or refusal on the part of an individual (A) interacting with another individual (B) to acknowledge B as a source of validation or nonvalidation places A in a paradoxical position: By failing to acknowledge another as a source of validation/nonvalidation, you invalidate or deprive yourself of your own worth. That is, by failing to acknowledge another person as a source of validation/nonvalidation, you deprive yourself of the possibility of being validated by another, and in so doing, you undermine your own self-worth or dignity. Individual dignity, therefore, is inextricably bound up in, is dependent on, the dignity of those with whom you interact. Or to state it more simply: to have dignity, you have to treat people with dignity.

Validation and Valuation Are Different Processes

Dignity is linked to, but it is not identical to, the valuation process. Validation, as previously noted, refers to the justification, ratification, or confirmation of our beliefs, emotions, and behaviors. As a result of repeated validation experiences, a personal belief in your worth emerges over time. This sense of worth gives rise to a predisposition to see yourself as a source of validation (or nonvalidation) for others. Thus, you learn over time through repeated validating and nonvalidating experiences that your perceptions, beliefs, and emotions are legitimate, defensible, and worthwhile sources of information about reality, and that they constitute a valid construction of reality that warrants acknowledgment. As you progress through childhood and into adulthood, if you have mostly validating experiences, and relatively fewer nonvalidating experiences, you come to believe that what you think or believe is generally worthwhile; it matters, and, in turn, you are worthwhile as well. You matter; you have dignity.

Conversely, to the extent that you do not develop a belief that you are a source of validation for others, a process will have been set in motion that will likely lead to the development of a predisposition to see yourself as being of little consequence or of having little worth. As a result of experiencing more nonvalidating interactions than validating ones, you may come to hold beliefs such as "It doesn't make any difference what I think" or "It doesn't make any difference whether I'm dead or alive." When you hold multiple beliefs such as these as an ongoing assessment of your consequence or worth, you will experience yourself as having little dignity.

The development over time of a personal sense of your dignity (or your lack thereof) shares much in common with the well-known idea of apperception. Within psychology, apperception refers to a process through which a new experience is taken in, is assimilated, and is influenced and transformed by coming into contact with your preexisting experience in a particular domain. This transformation leads to the creation of a new belief about the nature of reality. Apperceptions may also be influenced by the organizing and structuring influence of your thoughts regarding a specific aspect of your experience; in this case, your dignity.

Valuation, in contrast to validation, refers to the act of estimating or appraising the value or worth of some thing or event. Dignity's link to valuation is such that not valuing another person compromises that person as a source of validation for ourselves. Hence, not valuing another person renders that person's validation of little or no account. To be praised or invalidated by someone you consider incompetent, foolish, or worthless does little to change your own sense of worth. However, to be validated or not validated by someone you value highly may have considerable impact upon your sense of self-worth. Thus, to have dignity, you must be valued by others as well as value others; otherwise, their validation has no value for you.

Dignity as it is formulated here is functionally akin to Albert Bandura's (1977) concept of reciprocal determinism. Bandura states that people can influence their environment by acting in certain ways, and their changed environment will, in turn, influence their subsequent behavior.

As noted, failure or refusal on the part of individual A to engage in the validation process changes not only the outcome (the dignity) of individual B, but also the dignity of A as well. As it appears here, dignity takes on a more dynamic character than has been heretofore acknowledged. Rather than being an attributed or derivative characteristic, dignity emerges from a social psychological process that occurs as one individual interacts with another individual. The accretion, over time, of predominantly validating or nonvalidating interactions leaves a personal experiential deposit that we cognitively organize as our belief about our personal worth or dignity.

Dignity as a sense of self-worth, which arises from a validational process, shares a certain compatibility with some more traditional formulations seen within philosophy. For example, it has been widely suggested that to incarcerate or coerce people is to deprive them of their dignity. What appears to be meant here is that to restrict people's autonomy or self-expression in some sense impinges upon or deprives them of their dignity. Dignity as process is compatible with this formulation. The mutual and reciprocal validation/

nonvalidation that takes place during interpersonal interaction can only be authentic if each individual is free, not
constrained in any way, to engage in the validation process.
When we are forced to react to other people as if they were
valued, when indeed they are not, the validation process will
have been compromised. The individual participants, in this
case, will have diminished dignity.

Dignity as a Personal Sense of Worth

Dignity as process describes the dynamic experiential
flux from which personal worth emerges. How, though, does
this process become transformed into an individual's personal sense of worth? How, moreover, is it that some of us
will experience ourselves as having a greater or lesser sense
of self-worth than someone else? The means by which we
develop differentiated conceptions of self-worth is, again, a
process, and it is essentially the same process addressed in
self-theorist's accounts of the individuated and structural
act of self-conception (Fleming and Watts, 1980; Rosenberg,
1979; Shavelson, Hubner, and Stanton, 1976; Shavelson and
Bolus, 1982).

As part of the self-structure, your personal sense of worth
will emerge from the ongoing experience of differential consistencies with your environment; that is, with respect to dignity, the repeated validation or nonvalidation of specific expressions of personal experience. The experiential consistencies that result from interaction will be cognitively organized
over time into a belief of personal worth and will provide,

it is speculated, the structural underpinnings from which self-esteem, a related but distinct structure, will emerge. The widely known idea of apperception, a mental process in which you understand something you perceive in terms of previous experience, may afford additional clarity here.

More recent researchers (for example, Wouters et al., 2013; Crocker and Knight, 2006), while not focusing on the idea of dignity specifically, have sought to better understand self-worth by focusing on certain contingencies; that is, by focusing on the conditions upon which self-worth may depend. Examples include academic performance and athletic performance. Most of these efforts continue to treat our self-worth and our self-esteem as identical experiences. However, as previously described, these investigations measure our satisfaction with our role performance and competency, our self-esteem, rather than our dignity.

Other researchers (Cahill et al., 2007; McMahon, Felix, and Nagarajan, 2011; Antle, 2004) have similarly looked at contingencies of self-worth but have focused on more social experiences such as perceived social support, close friends, and support from parents. Such investigations appear more closely aligned with the idea of dignity as it is presented here. The common structural and functional element shared by these different forms of social support, and from which a personal sense of self-worth or dignity may emerge, appears to be the interdependent, reciprocal, and mutual process of validation that occurs during social interactions.

In view of what has been said thus far, a personal conception of self-worth or dignity results in the deep and abiding conviction that our existence makes a difference; a conviction that the totality of ourselves is worthy of affirmation.

Within the ongoing act of self-conception, dignity is here thought to occupy a foundational position within the self-structure. Self-esteem, an element within the self-structure frequently conflated with self-worth or dignity, is by contrast seen as being somewhat more peripheral. Dignity's place within the self-structure is thought to be so basic, so fundamental, that in most instances, it is axiomatic; that is, its existence is rarely (if ever) thought about or questioned. Accordingly, a person's sense of self-worth or dignity is conceived to be relatively stable over time and across situations, barring the most extraordinary of circumstances. Self-esteem, by contrast, is seen as being more situationally dependent and therefore subject to greater variability over time and across situations.

The difference between dignity and self-esteem may be further suggested by noting that each is a distinct but related element within the organizational act of self-conception. Dignity as a validation process is an interpersonal process and as such is reflexive and relational. Self-esteem, by contrast, is less frequently regarded to be either a relational or a reflexive construct. Personal satisfaction with your roles, performances, and competencies (self-esteem) need not necessarily involve either relational or reflexive considerations. As suggested, the validation process takes place through the

justification, ratification, and confirmation (or the nonjusti-
fication, nonratification, and nonconfirmation) of each inter-
actant's experience. To the extent that self-conception is an
expression of our individual experience, it is our sense of self
that is either validated or not validated, as our awareness of
ourselves emerges in presentation with another person and is
reflexively perceived through interaction with them. Frequent
and persistent nonvalidational experiences will likely lead to
structural reorganization of the self. A possible outcome of
such reorganization could be a diminished sense of dignity.

Self-esteem, by contrast, is seen as less socially dependent and therefore less reflexive, less relational in nature.
Self-esteem may derive from activities that are not social but
reflect success and competency within a specific situational
context or domain of activity. For example, failure to meet
a self-imposed standard (running a five-minute mile) could
contribute to a lower sense of self-esteem.

In agreement with numerous formulations, self-esteem is
seen here as both affective and evaluative in nature. Indeed,
the current presentation is in agreement with James Beane
and Richard Lipka's (1980) definition, which describes
self-esteem as "the personal satisfaction with roles and/or
quality of performance" (p. 2).

Feeling good or bad about the roles in which you engage
(being a parent, a friend, an elementary school teacher) or the
quality of your performances ("I did a good job") is not the
same thing as knowing that your existence has worth, that
you are an authentic source and reference point about reality

and interpersonal validation. Nor, indeed, is an awareness of our validational import the same thing as self-regard. It is possible, of course, that you may feel good or bad (esteem) about your validational status (worth), but the two, again, are not identical processes. Such distinctions can, of course, give rise to empirical investigations that may provide clarification within this long conflated area of belief.

An unfortunate but not uncommon experience you may have had may help clarify the difference between self-esteem and self-worth or dignity. From time to time, you may have found yourself involved in an activity that by your own admission was a worthless waste of time. The term "busywork" comes to mind. In a situation such as this, you may regard your efforts, the work, as essentially worthless because your exertions will not in any way validate the existence of another individual. As a consequence you, as the originator of the effort, receive no validation as well. A situation such as this undermines any possible validation of the needs or existence of the person who might have received the product of your efforts, or for yourself, the producer of the product. Because busywork provides no validation of either the person engaged in the busywork or anyone else, it confers no dignity on the worker or another person.

This view of self-worth recognizes that work is a viable and important avenue through which interpersonal validation and the establishment of dignity can occur. Again, however, the process by which this occurs is a social one. Validation will ordinarily take place because our efforts and their results affirm the needs and the existence of other human beings. The distinction between self-worth and self-esteem becomes clearer when we consider that the person providing the product in the busywork scenario may be especially adept, competent, and facile in the implementation of those duties. Indeed, the individual's satisfaction with his or her performance may be quite high. Thus, the job may contribute to a positive sense of self-esteem: "I did a good job." However, because the work has failed to provide validation of the needs of another person or the worker, it will not contribute to a sense of self-worth or dignity. In this case, the work confers no dignity upon the persons involved: "What a worthless waste of time this has been."

In the situation just described, it is important to appreciate that it is highly unlikely that one validating or nonvalidating experience will result in a noticeable change in our sense of dignity. Rather, over time and through the daily accretion of validating or nonvalidating experiences, we come to an understanding, a belief, regarding our individual worth in the world.

Given this difference between dignity and self-esteem, it becomes possible to describe situations in which individuals may be relatively successful and competent in their ongoing roles and activities. They may be relatively satisfied with their performance level, in other words, have adequate or high self-esteem. They may, nevertheless, have relatively low levels of self-worth, or dignity, because of the lack of validation they receive. The individual being described here is someone who may be seen as successful in the eyes of others, but who in that deep quiet place where all of us live our lives, feels that he or she is mostly worthless. These two items are on the Personal Worth Inventory (PWI, the self-report scale developed as part of my doctoral dissertation) to measure a person's sense of dignity: "I am worthless" and "It doesn't make any difference whether I am dead or alive." Some respondents indicated that these statements were mostly or completely true.

In a related vein, one of the populations included in the validation and reliability work when developing the PWI was a randomly selected sample of five hundred professors at the university I attended. The faculty members were contacted and requested to anonymously complete the PWI. Some of the questions on the scale apparently hit a nerve of one of the professors, who was sufficiently incensed by the items that he contacted my dissertation committee chairman and complained that the scale could not possibly measure anything and that I ought not to ask such questions of others. It may be that this particular professor, who in the eyes of the world would likely be seen as competent and in possession of a valued social role (status), was, nevertheless, troubled by the requirement to personally consider items like the two mentioned above (self-worth). There were not, by the way, similar expressions of anger from the other 499 faculty members contacted.

In another unexpected result involving the sample of five hundred university professors, no relationship was found between professorial rank and dignity as measured by the PWI. If social standing, status, is the basis for a personal sense of dignity, one would expect to find an increase in a professor's reported sense of dignity as his or her relative standing within the university community increased from assistant professor to associate professor to full professor. Relative standing within this status hierarchy was found to have no effect on a person's reported sense of dignity.

Differences between Dignity and Related Ideas
Dignity and Reward and Punishment

That one individual may be distinguished from another on the degree to which they see themselves having worth or dignity may be related, in part, to the individual's recognition that they act as a source of reward or punishment for others. Reward and punishment, in this context, do not refer to the extent to which someone may provide or withhold things wanted or unwanted by someone else, but rather it refers to the act of validating or not validating the actions, cognitions, and emotions of another. To validate, to confirm, and to accept another is generally experienced as rewarding. To invalidate, to reject, and to negate another is generally experienced to be punishing. These conditions hold true for the validator and the validated as well as the nonvalidator and the nonvalidated, as described earlier.

To describe the emergence of dignity as the result of a reward/cost operation is not to address the same phenomenon, however, covered by George Homans' (1961) concept of inter- personal value. In referring to the value of actions as they occur in interpersonal interchanges, Homans stated that the value of a unit of behavior may be positive or negative. It is the degree of reinforcement or punishment one receives for a behavior that determines its value. Although dignity is conceived to arise through acts that share some of the attributes of reward and punishment, it is not the same thing as merely giving reward or punishment.

Dignity and Power

When we interact with one another, we wield immense power. This is especially the case with regard to the validation and invalidation process. Indeed, we create dignity anew each time we interact with another person. This reference to power is generally in keeping with John Thibaut and Harold Kelly's (1959) formulation of power in which power is seen to result when two persons interact in such a fashion that "each person has the possibility of affecting the other's reward/cost position and thereby influencing or controlling him" (p. 100). The validation/nonvalidation process is also congruent with Thibaut and Kelly's account of "fate control": the degree to which others can determine one's outcomes no matter what one does.

It is perhaps stating the obvious to note that it would be difficult to experience ourselves as having dignity and at the same time to experience ourselves as being powerless and ineffectual. To have a personal sense of dignity is not simply to have a sense of power, however. Nor can dignity be adequately explained away by simply referring to the sum of our personal reinforcement and punishment history. Our sense of worth results from the extent to which our experience has, in the past, been validated; therefore, we have a personal sense of being a source of validation for others. In other words, the experience of dignity is qualitatively different from the sum of the events that give rise to it.

Our personal sense of dignity is an assumption, a belief about reality. This sense of worth emerges not only from an awareness of our capacity to affect another's outcomes but also from an awareness to literally affect the ground of another's being. In other words, to determine what another is. In a very literal sense, when two individuals are in interaction with one another, they are not only co-creators of each other's outcomes, they are co-creators of each other. Dignity, then, is created, is an emergent property that takes place when two individuals interact with one another, and in the absence of interaction, it does not exist. To the extent that individuals have become aware, either explicitly or otherwise, of the importance they play in the interpersonal process, they will experience a sense of personal worth or dignity. To the extent that such an awareness is absent, a personal sense of dignity will be absent.

A fundamental aspect of the social interdependence inherent in human dignity is its omnipresent and continuous operation when two human beings are in the presence of one another. In other words, we cannot help co-creating one another's experience through validation or *"See* Burke" invalidation, in much the same way that we cannot help communicating with another person, whether we want to or not, when we are in their presence. Whether we acknowledge or purposely ignore another person, communication and thus information is exchanged. Similarly, whether we consciously and deliberately acknowledge (validate) or purposely ignore another person (invalidate), dignity is nevertheless augmented or diminished. The validation or invalidation process is simply one of the things that happens when an individual is aware of the presence of another individual.

Dignity and Interactionist Theory

The current formulation of dignity/worth seems generally compatible with Peter Burk's (1980) work in the area of interactionist theory and particularly applicable to the role the meaning of behavior plays in self-conception. Burke espouses an interdependent, reflexive, and relational view of self-conception by referring to personal identity (the internal component of a role), self-image (the current working copy of the identity as it is applied to in vivo exchanges), and behavior when he states, "Performance is thus the externalization of the image in the sense that the meanings of the behaviors in the performance are the meaning of the self-contained in the image" (p. 21).

George H. Mead (1934) offered an earlier and similar position when he noted, "The meanings of the self are learned by the person because others respond as if the person had an identity appropriate to that particular role performance."

Such responses provide cues to appropriate role performance and, by implication, to an appropriate identity for one who performs in appropriate ways. In this fashion, one's actions develop meaning through the reactions of others and, over time, gradually call up in the person the responses that are called up in others.

Such is the case with dignity. If dignity may be thought of as the meaning that follows from the validational process, then a personal conception of worth will develop over time as one's actions develop meaning (worth) through the reactions of others (validation) and gradually call up in the person the responses (dignity) that are called up on others.

Measurement

Dignity as a process of reciprocal validation is additionally successful in meeting most of the measurement requirements outlined by Burke (1980) as necessary when using an interactive approach to the self. The measurement requirements are based upon six theoretical properties of the self, as seen from an interactionist perspective. The theoretical properties and their relationship to dignity are offered below.

(The more general reader who may have less interest in detailed technical issues within psychology can easily skip the following section without diminishing their understanding of the general aspects of dignity.)

(1) The self is composed of an organized set of identities. George McCall and J. L. Simmons (1966) and Sheldon

Stryker (1968) have suggested that identities relate to one another via a salience hierarchy. All things being equal, a given identity, relative to other identities, will be utilized or evoked in a particular situation depending upon its place within the salience hierarchy. Those identities high within the salience hierarchy are more likely to be evoked in more situations than those lower in the hierarchy. Dignity may be seen as an organized aspect of identity that obtains prominence within the salience hierarchy: an identity that is present in more situations than many other identity constituents.

(2) Identities are self-in-role meanings. As already mentioned, one of the principal meanings of the social validation process is worth, and worth as an aspect of self-identity inheres in the reciprocal ratification, confirmation, and justification of social intercourse.

(3) Identities are defined relationally in terms of counter-identities. To perceive ourselves as having worth will allow us to see ourselves as being a source of validation/nonvalidation for others. To the extent that we fail or are disinclined to engage in validational experiences with another, that person will be deprived of the meaning that accrues from validation and hence experience an identity with a diminished sense of worth.

(4) Identities are reflexive. Burke (1980) sees reflexivity as feedback to the self, regarding the consequence of the processes that are the self. Dignity accommodates

this requirement nicely. When we deprive another of dignity by failure to validate or by nonvalidation, and thus define another as an invalid source of validation, we deprive ourselves of our own dignity by depriving ourselves of possible validation by another.

(5) Identities operate indirectly. Here, Burke argues that identities are a kind of idealized picture of the self-in-role which provides the motivation for performance through the mediation of labile constructions called self-images. These presumably guide moment-to-moment interaction with others. To hold the deep and abiding certainty that you are worthy, versus the deep and abiding certainty that you are not worthy, is likely to differentially influence the moment-to-moment interactions you have with others.

(6) Identities motivate social behavior. Nelson Foote (1951) suggested that one of the primary functions of an identity is motivation. According to Foote, identity defines a problematic situation as calling for performance of a particular act with more or less anticipated consequences. Then the energy appropriate to performing the necessary action will be released. In the broadest sense, all interactions possess the potential for validating or nonvalidating outcomes. However, there are numerous instances when validation might be seen to specifically express the motivational element proposed by Burke. Depending on its degree,

a felt lack of self-worth worth could motivate a person to undertake interaction with another in search of validation and an improved sense of self-worth. Persons with extremely low self-worth might avoid interactions because they feel they have little to contribute that would be accepted by another individual. Conversely, individuals with a sense of high self-worth might undertake interactions to enhance the feelings of worth in another by validation or to enhance their own feeling of worth by validation of another. It seems unlikely that persons with a genuine sense of high self-worth (dignity) would be motivated to invalidate another person. Such behavior will be more likely to be seen in individuals with speciously high self-regard (esteem) or in individuals attempting to assert their worth at the expense of others.

The circumstances as described above seem to lead to asymmetrical predictions regarding the motivational significance of dignity as a psychological construct. On the one hand, low self-worth may lead to interaction, or it may inhibit interaction. On the other hand, high self-worth may lead to interaction but not inhibit interaction. A contributing element that may clarify predictions is the valuation, as previously noted, one individual holds regarding the validation of the other individual. Because dignity is an interactive process, it is necessary to consider the personal perceptions of worth and valuation of each person and the person's perception of their co-interactant's valuation and worth when making predictions regarding the initiation or inhibition of behavior. In general, however, it seems likely that persons who experience low self-worth will find the condition uncomfortable and will undertake actions to reduce their discomforting state of affairs.

The Components of Dignity

Implicit in the foregoing, dignity has both a personal and an extrapersonal component (another individual's personal experience). The personal component gives rise to cognitive organization within our own self-structure, as well as a relatively stable perception of dignity, or lack thereof, across different situations. As previously suggested, this organization and resultant structuring arise from the validation/nonvalidation we receive from others through our interactions with them. The extrapersonal component corresponds to the interactions we have with others and results from the experience of worth we create in others through the validation/ nonvalidation of those individuals and the validation/nonvalidation we receive from them. As an emergent psychological phenomenon, dignity helps to understand how our personal worth depends on the worth of the people with whom we interact and vice versa.

Dignity and Behavior

The realization of dignity that validation provides finds its ultimate expression in our behavior as we dispense and receive rewards (validation) and costs (nonvalidation) during our interpersonal exchanges. When we validate another person during an interaction, we affirm not only the worth and existence of the other person, their dignity, we also affirm our own worth and existence as a source of validation, our own dignity. Alternatively, when we invalidate another individual during interaction, we diminish the worth of the other person, their dignity, but we seemingly enhance our own worth and existence as a source of nonvalidation. The expression of nonvalidation in the interpersonal process will most likely be seen in maladaptive and defensive interactions in which individuals attempt to assert their worth, as a source of invalidation, at the expense of another by ignoring, belittling, or demeaning the other person. This type of behavior is, of course, self-defeating because reducing the worth of someone else reduces our own worth as well.

Finally, when we refuse or fail to provide either validation or invalidation of another person altogether, and in so doing withhold another's dignity, we ultimately deny our own worth by failing to express either aspect of our potential as a source of validation or invalidation. Such a condition might follow from circumstances in which the potential existed for interaction between two persons, but the interaction never materialized, perhaps because of hostility, indifference, or lack of awareness.

Dignity and Suicide

Another behavioral situation in which dignity may be thought to play an important role is suicide. Dignity as a personal sense of worth may play an important role in certain situations involving suicide, particularly suicide among the elderly. Physical debility or chronic disease aside, many elderly persons, in the absence of productive job-related activities, may no longer find adequate personal validation to support their continued existence. They may no longer receive validation from age cohorts, friends, and family members who may have died. Moreover, elderly individuals may experience diminished validation in response to a society that finds little use for or interest in their abilities and concerns. In such circumstances as these, individuals may opt for suicide as a means for coping with a perceived existence of interminable nonvalidation or worthlessness. Indeed, it can be speculated that one reason news of suicide affects us so deeply is precisely because suicide seemingly invalidates the ongoing efforts and aspirations of the living. That is, suicide may be seen by those remaining as a rejection of their value for life. Similarly, there is a sense in which as a suicide occurs, living persons are diminished in some small measure because all persons have been deprived of a potential source of validation; they have been deprived to a small degree of their own dignity. Thus, there may be an implicit and a tacit recognition of one's own diminution through the loss of others that accounts for the power the news of suicide exerts over many people.

5

Research Findings Thus Far

I n addition to a personal interest, my principal reason for undertaking an inquiry into the topic of dignity was to fulfill the dissertation requirement for the doctoral degree in psychology at Virginia Commonwealth University. Beyond the initial historical overview and the theoretical development on the origin of dignity, the majority of effort was directed toward developing an instrument, a scale, which would be a reliable and valid measure of a person's sense of self-worth or dignity. To that end, approximately a thousand individuals from various population groups participated in the development of the Personal Worth Inventory (PWI) scale. The resultant PWI is a twenty-five-item, factor analytically derived self-report scale that measures a person's sense of dignity.

Individuals who participated in the development of the PWI completed the dignity scale in addition to a number of other widely used and well-regarded self-report inventories. Following various statistical analyses of the participant group's answers, a number of anticipated results were found, as well as results that were a surprise.

In reviewing the results of this data-gathering project, it is important to keep in mind that the findings, as they are described here, do not constitute inviolable truth. They instead should be cautiously regarded as initial and exploratory findings that may point to potentially illuminating and significant aspects of a person's experience of dignity as well as provide evidence that supports (or does not support) my analysis of dignity's origin.

Gender

A finding that is likely in line with most people's expectations is that no relationship was found between dignity and gender. That is, women were found to have no more dignity nor less dignity than men do, and men were found to have no more dignity nor less dignity than women do. An intriguing question on which future research could shed light is whether the absence of a relationship between dignity and gender holds true for cultures in which equality is a value not as prominently held as it is in the United States.

As the stomachs of some readers are likely beginning to turn as they read this, it is perhaps important to keep in mind that the origin of dignity, as it is described here, is an interpersonal co-creation. It is the result of individual experience. Because dignity is the result of experience, some people will have experiences that lead to a greater sense of dignity, and others will have experiences that will result in a lesser sense of dignity. All of this is to say that because dignity is the result of experience, it is learned. And by modifying a person's experience, their sense of dignity can be modified as well.

Race

An additional finding that will likely not lead to much controversy is that no relationship was found between dignity and race. That is, no racial group that was included in the study was found to have more or less dignity than another racial group.

Age

A finding that was not anticipated is the curvilinear relationship between dignity and age. Based on the data gathered, dignity appears to increase as we advance in age until around sixty-five years of age, after which it begins to decline. The reason for this pattern is likely the result of the contribution of a number of factors, each of which contribute to the power our social experience has in molding our self-conceptions.

One possible reason a person's sense of dignity may diminish around the age of sixty-five is related to their retirement from the work force. At the time these data were gathered, sixty-five was the widely assumed age at which many individuals in the United States began to leave the work force. Greater variability in retirement onset may be seen currently, given changes in national economic and health conditions, and these changes may in turn lead to greater variability in the age of a worker's departure from the work force than was previously seen. In any case, work is, for most of us, an important experience that contributes substantially to our sense of self-worth. Indeed, it is through our occupational efforts that we validate the needs and existence of other human beings, and in turn their appreciation of our efforts validates our contributions. In earlier years, when I was still a university professor, I would often introduce this finding in my social psychology lectures as a point of discussion. A number of older students, who had returned to school following their retirement, emphatically endorsed the interpretation suggested by dignity theory. They acknowledged that one of the more challenging aspects of adapting to life following retirement was their loss of the sense of worth they had known during the years they were engaged in work.

Another consideration that increasingly becomes a reality for many of us as we enter the later years of our lives, and which may contribute to a reduction in our sense of dignity, involves the loss of friends, age cohorts, and family members who have died. Frequently referred to as "social support networks," the presence of other individuals with whom we share supportive and validating relationships is known to have beneficial effects on our well-being and longevity. In the absence of our former validating interactions, a diminution in our felt sense of dignity is sadly a reality for too many. Indeed, it is not too hard to imagine an elderly person living alone without friends or family, perhaps meagerly getting by on Social Security, with infrequent and mostly utilitarian interactions with others. It is further not too difficult to imagine that an individual in such circumstances might respond to the PWI item "It doesn't make any difference whether I am dead or alive" as being completely true or mostly true for them. Some individuals who completed the PWI during my data gathering endorsed this item as being completely true or mostly true for themselves.

An additional factor that may contribute to people's waning sense of dignity in their later years of life is found in our culture's failure to value our elderly. As a nation, we tend to terminate the social role of our elderly long before their biological role ends. Our often misdirected over-valuation of the latest and the new at the expense of what has preceded it tends to cast the new as preferable and more desirable, and that which preceded it as less so, if not inferior and obsolete.

A future research question that could prove relevant and illuminating is whether a similar loss of age-related dignity is seen in persons who live in collectivistic culturess", such as those seen in Asia, Central and South America, and Africa, rather than in individualistic cultures such as the United States. Collectivistic cultures are ones in which greater value is given to the needs and goals of the group rather than those of the individual. Collectivistic cultures tend to promote unity, selflessness, and community needs above the needs of the individual.

Individualistic cultures, by contrast, place greater value on the interests of the individual person rather than the interests of the group. Individualistic cultures promote independence, assertiveness, self-identity, and the rights and concerns of each person over the interests of the group.

During the dissertation project's data-gathering phase, this author informally observed that a small subsample of Asian respondents unanimously indicated complete agreement with two of the PWI items that were specifically included to assess the interdependent and reciprocal nature of dignity: "The way other people treat me has a role to play in how I view myself" and "My value in life depends upon how I treat other people." Respondents from more traditionally Western orientations were found to typically indicate only moderate agreement with these two PWI items. Indeed, the overall correlation between the personal worth and the extra-personal worth subscales was a moderate .51. This may seem rather underwhelming empirical support for dignity theory's central tenet: that self-worth is dependent upon the dignity of others. Strong evidence for such a hypothesized relationship would be expected to be closer to 1.0 The finding, however, may reflect the influence of an individualist cultural orientation shared by the majority of the participants in the study, for whom awareness of the interdependence of dignity is not a prominent and culturally shared belief.

Given collectivistic culture's tendency to counter self-interests in deference to the interests of the group, and the reflexive and reciprocal conditions from which dignity emerges, the age-related waning of dignity in one's later years of life may not be as pronounced within groups that share a collectivistic orientation. Such speculations can, of course, be clarified by further research. Indeed, many fascinating questions and potential clarifications are suggested by the initial results.

Clinical Group

Another intriguing finding that must be regarded as provisionally exploratory, owing to its small sample size, involves individuals who presented themselves at Virginia Commonwealth University Counseling Services and Psychological Counseling Services, also at VCU. It was hypothesized that persons seeking professional counseling services were likely undergoing personal distress and that an aspect of their distress might involve a reduced sense of self-worth or dignity.

When the PWI responses of persons in the clinical sample were compared to the responses of persons in a nonclinical sample (individuals not seeking professional mental health services), some dramatic differences were seen. In the nonclinical group, a positive relationship was found between the two PWI items: "I take other people's feelings into consideration before responding," and "The way other people treat me has a role to play in how I view myself." Each of these items were conceived to be dignity-affirmative statements, and endorsement of either statement was taken as evidence of beliefs contributing to an individual's sense of self-worth. The positive correlational relationship between the two statements essentially means that as a person's endorsement of one statement increases, their endorsement of the other statement also increases, and conversely, as their endorsement of the first statement decreases, their endorsement of the second statement also decreases.

By contrast, in the clinical group, a negative correlation (relationship) was found between the same two items. That is, as a person's agreement with one of the statements increased, their endorsement of the other statement decreased.

It is not my intention to present a detailed research report here by laying out all the ways in which the clinical group's responses were the inverse of the nonclinical group. I would like, however, to include one additional example to provide readers with a fuller sense of the inner life of the individuals who were sufficiently distressed to seek professional help.

A negative correlation was additionally found between another pair of PWI items in the clinical sample: "The way other people treat me has a role to play in how I view myself" and "My value in life depends on how I treat other people." As is likely obvious, each of these statements was included in the questionnaire to capture the interdependent and reciprocal element of dignity's origin, as outlined within this book.

The negative correlation demonstrates that as a respondent's endorsement of the first statement increased, their endorsement of the second statement decreased, and conversely, as their endorsement of the first statement decreased, their endorsement of the second statement increased. In other words, respondents were saying, "The more I believe the way other people treat me has a role to play in how I view myself, the less I believe my value in life depends on how I treat other people me," and conversely, "The more I believe my value in life depends on how I treat other people, the less I believe the way other people treat me has a role to play in how I view myself."

While it is possible that a substantial number of US citizens, because of our culture's individualistic orientation, may not consciously realize the interdependent nature of our worth, and thus hold the kind of incompatible beliefs represented by the examples of PWI items reported above, the felt tension that such mutually incompatible beliefs produce, and which ultimately are expressed in the nature and quality of the interpersonal relationships we have with others, may provide some insight into the distress that initially brought members of the clinical sample to seek professional assistance. Further, their need to access clinical services, when viewed through the lens of dignity theory, suggests that their distress may have arisen from their attempt to assert their worth as sources of invalidation in their relationship(s) with others: a practice that is always self-defeating, and in so doing, they experienced the distress of a diminution in their own dignity as well.

By contrast, responses to these same items did not result in negative correlations when the PWI's intercorrelation matrix was examined for the nonclinical sample. In fact, no negative correlations were found within the nonclinical sample.

Self-Esteem

One final outcome that may be of some interest to general readers, and of particular interest to specialists, involves the previously mentioned conflation regarding self-esteem and self-worth, and a finding supporting the distinctiveness of each concept. When the answers of respondents who completed the PWI, the dignity scale, were compared with the same respondents' answers to two well-known and widely used self-esteem scales, weak positive correlations were found between the self-esteem scales and the dignity scale. If the self-esteem scale and the dignity scale had been measuring the same thing, the relationship between them would have been expected to be considerably stronger or approaching 1.0 (perfect correspondence between the two scales). Inasmuch as the correspondence between the two concepts, dignity and self-esteem, was weak, in the .30s, this finding provides evidence in support of the earlier claim that self-worth, or dignity, and self-esteem are not the same thing. Having worth and being an authentic source of validation or nonvalidation regarding reality, dignity, is different from the satisfaction or dissatisfaction you feel, an emotion, regarding your role performances and competencies.

6

Intersubjective Validation

The intersubjective process of validation (or invalidation) from which human dignity emerges (or is suppressed) not only impacts your self-concept, the beliefs you hold regarding yourself, which is also that aspect of human experience with which much of psychology has been concerned, it also impacts your ontology: your being in the world.

Validation or invalidation is in a sense the respective green or red light that says in essence, "Yes, come forth," or "No, stay away." That is, the experience of intersubjective validation is a fundamental, a radical acknowledgment of being, and it is not mere agreement or disagreement with the ideas, feelings, or behaviors expressed by another person during social interaction. Validation is acknowledgment and acceptance of the consciousness embodied in another individual to express in phenomenal creation as social interaction. Thus, not only is the individual's self-concept influenced, that is, their beliefs about who they are, but the being, the worth, of the individual—the individual's presence—as it is expressed, is manifested through behavior that is also influenced. Behavior in this context includes, of course, verbal behavior, speech, gestures, signs, books about dignity, and so on.

Desideratum

In previous public presentations on the topic of dignity, with its central focus on the process of validation, and my earlier assertion that apart from interaction, dignity does not exist, I have been sometimes asked what role (if any) animal companions, aka pets, might play in the creation of dignity. Because this is likely an idea that may have occurred to some readers, a few thoughts may be welcome here.

First of all, let me say that this topic is one on which, to my knowledge, no research has yet been conducted. Thus, my comments here are suppositions based on my observations, the observations of others, and my familiarity with the topic of the creation of individual worth. It seems to me, in any case, that this is a topic about which future investigation might yield fascinating results.

At issue is the question of whether or not human interactions with nonhuman entities result in an enhancement or diminution of individual worth, and whether or not validation is the mechanism by which the worth is created. As the process of validation and the emergence of worth is most broadly applied, it seems to me, that the answer to this question is likely yes. The extent to which validation may occur, however, seems a matter of degree, and the degree will in all likelihood vary with the level of consciousness, mutuality, and capacity for reciprocal interaction between the two beings involved. To the extent the foregoing is accurate, the potential for the creation of the most significant degrees of dignity will likely take place between one human interacting with another human. This statement should not be construed to mean that beings other than humans are somehow inferior or categorically deficient in worth or incapable of contributing to the creation of worth. Instead, as the phylogenetic distance between humans and other entities increases, our ability to assess their reactions and, more particularly, their internal experience is, at this time, correspondingly limited (if not nonexistent).

The preceding considerations notwithstanding, anecdotal evidence passionately and vehemently affirmed by countless legions of pet owners over extensive periods of time attests to the belief that substantial contributions to a caretaker's personal sense of worth results from their involvement with their animal companions. In addition to providing caretakers with a number of life-affirming experiences such as a sense of purpose, a sense of responsibility, love, and companionship, animal companions contribute to the validation of their caretakers' worth by their confirmation of their actions on their behalf through their acceptance, benefit, and flourishing.

What Difference Does All This Make?

Shifts in established ways of thinking can be difficult to make. History is replete with dramatic examples of how established ways of thinking have been met with intense resistance, hostility, and sometimes even violence. This seems particularly the case when our beliefs about the fundamental nature of reality are called into question. Consider the now familiar case of Nicolaus Copernicus who, in the 1500s, when most believed that the earth was the center of the universe, proposed that the earth moved around the sun. It took almost one hundred years for his ideas to begin to be taken seriously. Indeed, when Galileo Galilei, following on Copernicus' work, claimed in 1632 that the earth orbited the sun, he was placed under house arrest for committing heresy against the Catholic church.

Or consider the case of Charles Darwin, who in 1859 published *On the Origin of Species,* in which he proposed a theory of biological evolution based on natural selection: a process by which organisms change over time in response to changes in their environment. Darwin's theory has received more scientific verification than most major theories, yet there are people who continue to reject his findings as an inaccurate account of the world.

Another example of existing beliefs reluctantly giving way to more incisive descriptions of the nature of the world can be seen in the current controversy over the role, if any, humans play in global changes in weather. Accumulating evidence and the passage of time will likely contribute to a gradual change in the public's view of the role human behavior plays in the shifts seen in the earth's weather patterns. For now, however, conflicting beliefs remain firmly held.

By introducing these examples, I do not presume to imagine that the ideas presented here are likely to produce similar epoch-changing shifts in human thinking. They are offered as well-known and acknowledged examples of how widely held beliefs can incur vigorous resistance in their protracted journey to more widely embraced acceptance.

What then is likely to change if the idea that dignity is created through a process of reciprocal, and interdependent validation when a person interacts with another person becomes widely accepted? The short answer is: not much, and a great deal.

Should acceptance become widespread, the world will likely continue to spin on its axis as it has for billions of years, and people will continue to do pretty much what we have been doing for millions of years. The most significant difference will be that more of us will have an accurate idea of where our dignity comes from and, because of that, what we are doing (co-creating one another) when we interact with each other. Because of this awareness, we will be able to more consciously and deliberately engage in the process of our own creation and the creation of others. And we will be more aware of what our actions potentially mean for the dignity of another person and for the dignity of ourselves, as well.

To a considerable extent, the development and perpetuation of dignity has been implicit in the numerous mores and norms seen in all cultures, to which most of us have been exposed throughout our lives. From our earliest days, we have been encouraged to refrain from giving offense to others through either word or gesture. The extensive history of manners, seen in every culture, has evolved with the specific intention of taking the other person into account through our actions and words, and promoting a felicitous relationship that honors the other person. Certainly, the golden rule of treating others as we would wish to be treated has found acceptance in numerous cultures throughout the world, and it stands as one of the clearest and most concise means by which dignity can be created and sustained.

With an informed awareness of the origins of dignity, we might conceivably behave more ethically in our dealings with one another, as we come to realize and accept that to diminish another person is to diminish ourselves and to do so is self-defeating. Some of us will likely not care that this is the case, and we will continue to assert ourselves as sources of invalidation in our mistaken belief that the diminution of others enhances our own being. Such persons would be seen as possessing less dignity because of their actions, and correspondingly, they would experience less dignity. The expression of self-righteous indignation through the invalidation of others just might become less tenable. When, however, has harming, belittling, or demeaning someone ever been seen as dignified behavior? Even though individuals who engage in such behavior would cause diminished validation following from the invalidation of others, their self-esteem might, nevertheless, remain mostly unaffected, as described earlier, due to their success in the particular arena of their endeavor;

in other words, their satisfaction with their role performance or competency could remain high.

Governmental and legal champions of human dignity will continue to have a defensible basis for affirming the centrality of dignity in human experience, while inveighing against behavior that fails to value the worth of other human beings. Affronts to human dignity, a human's dignity, will continue to provide an argument against conscious and intentional harm directed toward another. However, the argument against harm will not derive from the violation of a transcendent religious precept nor a rejection of the distillation of centuries of social usage and precedent. Instead, dignity, which some have argued does not exist, will be more widely known to indeed exist in the emergent quality and nature of the behavior that accrues for human involvement with one another. The case for infringements of dignity will be defensibly and organically strengthened in a way that was previously unavailable.

In a related matter, it will continue to be possible to compellingly argue, as it has been attempted in the past, that human beings have a right to their dignity. Humans have a right to anything that governments, legal structures, and societies are willing to affirm, but to argue that humans do not have a right to dignity, in view of dignity theory as presented here, is like arguing that humans do not have a right to breathe, and if that is the case, all bets are off. Simply stated: We can hardly help having dignity, although some of us may be more successful at creating or destroying it than others.

The precepts guiding dignity within medicine and nursing, as well as other caregiving and professional arenas, will continue to be as relevant and essential as they are at present. The most likely difference may be in the practitioner's realization that treating a client or patient with dignity does not depend upon the ritualized and formulaic interjection of prescribed words and behavior, but instead it emerges from being fully present to and conscious of the moment-to-moment, reciprocal, and interdependent potential for validation during the professional interchange.

A personal example from the early years of my professional career may help illustrate essential aspects of the dignity-making process during such interactions. My introduction to working with persons with developmental disabilities occurred in a state-supported residential center in the mid-1980s. My patients were mostly severely and profoundly retarded individuals (as they were called at the time) in a severe maladaptive behavior unit. They were developmentally functioning at a nonverbal level, and they exhibited severe, aggressive, or self-injurious behavior such as breaking bones, pulling out rectums and eyeballs, and destroying property. As someone who had never imagined that such a shocking and profound level of disability could possibly exist, I was overwhelmed. I was overwhelmed with sorrow for their condition, and I was overwhelmed by the seemingly impossible task I had before me. I quickly came to realize, however, that my sorrow was not helping me or my clients, and I instead plunged into my daunting responsibilities with all the vigor and determination that a shiny new PhD psychologist could muster.

It turned out well for a number of my clients, even those who functioned at a developmental level of one year old; they taught me that no matter how low they may have been in a social status hierarchy, they possessed in abundance the capacity to validate my presence. In so doing, they gave my life value and dignity that no one before or since has surpassed. In turn, my efforts to address their needs validated their existence and gave their life dignity, as well.

Another area that figures prominently in recent discussions is the issue of death with dignity and the implicit matter of self-directed or assisted suicide. Dignity theory as described in this offering will not, I believe, substantially alter the controversy surrounding this passionately argued issue. This is largely due to the proponents of so-called death with dignity, and its opponents, anchoring their arguments in different reference points of valuation. Proponents of death with dignity, those who support the self-directed or assisted termination of one's own life, generally see its essential value inhering in the individual person and their validation of the individual's prerogative to end their human experience as a responsible, autonomous, and sentient being. This is in contrast to the end of someone's human experience where the individual is incapable of autonomy, reason, or making decisions for themselves. Opponents of death with dignity often see the essential value at issue inhering in transcendent moral or cultural precepts *about* the life in question. Their

argument is more about life in general, as a reified phenomenon, and less about the individual person in question. The
origin of such an argument is seemingly derived from a more
transcendent viewpoint; it usually does not originate with a
specific person.

In view of such considerations, dignity theory appears
more aligned with the view held by the death with dignity
supporters. The now familiar interdependent and reciprocal
validation outlined here, and implicit in the death with dignity position, affirms the centrality of the individual person's
experience and constitutes, in this particular instance, a felicitous alliance.

As suggested earlier, the privileging of reified and abstract
conceptions is a tradition that has for too long conflated is
with ought, and it has misled countless generations into confusion and unnecessary unhappiness.

Thus, it is with an interest in our individual and collective
condition as human beings, and a desire to understand each
more accurately and clearly, that this account of dignity is
offered. I'm presenting these ideas through the medium of a
book because that format can reach the most people interested in knowing more about this topic, more particularly
those who felt uncomfortable with previous explanations regarding dignity's origin. These thoughts on dignity, I believe,
are of sufficient centrality and significance that they should
not languish in a little-read journal seen only by the eyes of
a few specialists.

As my research into what has been said about dignity has continued in the years following my initial work on the topic, I have come to be immensely impressed with the intelligence, the care, and the commitment writers have brought to a critically important aspect of the condition of being human. Some of what earlier writers and thinkers have contributed to our current understanding of dignity has been included here as a way of showing how we have come to hold our present beliefs about dignity. Additionally, this book has attempted to provide an account of dignity at its most elemental level, that is, as an individual person's experience of worth. As a psychological experience, human worth, originally recognized as individual excellence, has been implicit throughout dignity's venerable evolution to its present-day understanding. Now with an awareness of dignity's emergence through a psychological process of social validation, we can today consciously and with intention benefit from the message that millennia of human interaction has continuously and quietly whispered: To have dignity, you have to treat people with dignity.

References

Antle, Beverley J. (2004). Factors associated with self-worth in young people with physical disabilities. *Health & Social Work, 29,* 3, 167–175.

Aquinas, Thomas (1997). *Scriptum Super Libros Sententiarium (Aquinas on Creation)*, trans. Steven E. Baldner and Willian E. Carrol. Toronto: Pontifical Institute of Mediaeval Studies.

Battista, M. (1975). *St. Thomas Aquinas' Philosophy: in the Commentary to the Sentences.* Netherlands: The Hague.

Bean, J. A., and Lipka, R. P. (1980). Self-concept and self-esteem: a construct differentiation. *Child Study Journal, 10,* 106.

Berger, L., and Luckman, T. (1967). *The Social Construction of Reality.* Garden City, NY: Doubleday.

Blackhart, G., Nelson, B., Knowles, M., and Baumeister, R. (2009). Rejection elicits emotional reactions but neither causes immediate distress nor lowers self-esteem: A meta-analytic review of 192 studies on social exclusion. *Personality & Social Psychology Review, 13,* 4, 269–309.

Brownfain, J. (1952). Stability of the self-concept as a dimension of personality. *Journal of Abnormal and Social Psychology, 47,* 596–606.

Burke, P. J. (1980). The self: Measurement requirements from an interactionist perspective. *Social Psychology Quarterly, 43,* 1, 18–29.

Burns, R. B. (1979). *The Self-Concept.* London: Longman.

Burwell, R. A. (2006). Self processes in adolescent depressions: The role of self-worth contingencies. *Journal of Research on Adolescence, 16,* 3, 479–490.

Chang, H. (1980). Neo-Confucian moral thought and its moral legacy. *The Journal of Asian Studies, 39* (2): 259–277.

Cicero, M. T. (1991). *On Duties.* E. M. Atkins (ed.), trans. M. T. Griffin. Cambridge: Cambridge University Press.

Cooley, C. H. (1902). *Human Nature and the Social Order.* New York: Charles Scribner & Sons.

Coopersmith, S. (1967). *The Antecedents of Self-Esteem.* San Francisco: W. H. Freeman.

Crocker, J., and Knight, K. M. (2005). Contingencies of self-worth. *America Psychological Society, 14,* 4, 200–203.

Dobson, C., Goudy, W. J., Keith, P. M., and Powers, E. (1979). Further analysis of Rosenberg's self-esteem scale. *Psychological Reports, 44,* 639–641.

Crandall, R. (1973). "The measurement of self-esteem and related constructs." In Robinson and Shaver (Eds.), *Measures of Social Psychological Attitudes.* Ann Arbor: Michigan Institute for Social Research.

Darwin, C. (1964). *On the Origin of Species: A Facsimile of the First Edition.* Cambridge, Massachusetts and London, England: Harvard University Press.

Diggory, J. C. (1966). *Self-Evaluation-Concepts and Studies.* New York: Wiley.

Erol, R. Y., and Orth, U. (2011). Self-esteem development from age 14 to 30 years: A longitudinal study. *Journal of Personality & Social Psychology, 101,* 607–619.

Fitts, W. H. (1965). *Tennessee Self-Concept Scale.* Nashville: Counselor Recordings and Tests.

Fleming, J. S., and Watts, W. A. (1980). The dimensionality of self-esteem: Some results of a college sample. *Journal of Personality and Social Psychology, 39,* 5, 921–929.

Forsyth, D., Lawrence, N., Burnette, J., and Baumeister, R. (2007). Attempting to improve the academic performance of struggling college students by bolstering their self-esteem: An intervention that backfired. *Journal of Social & Clinical Psychology, 26,* 4, 447–459.

Gadin, K. G., and Hammarstrom, A. (2003). Do changes in the psychosocial school environment influence pupil's health development? Results from a three-year follow-up study. *Scandinavian Journal of Public Health, 31,* 3, 169.

Gergen, K. (1971). *The Concept of Self.* New York: Holt, Rinehart & Winston.

Giovanni Pico della Mirandola (1956). *Oration on the Dignity of Man,* trans. A. R. Caponigri. Washington, DC: Regnery Gateway.

Gushee, D. P. (2013). A Christian Theological Account of Human Worth. In C. McCrudden (Ed.) *Understanding Human* Dignity (pp. 275-288). London: Oxford University Press.

Harter, S., Waters, P., and Whitesell, N. R. (1998). Relational self-worth: Differences in perceived worth as a person across interpersonal contexts among adolescents. *Child Development, 69,* 756–766.

Hume, D. *Treatise on Human Nature.* (1739-1740). (Ed.) L. A. Selby-Bigge. Oxford: Clarendon, 1951.

James, W. (1988). *Principles of Psychology* (Vol. 1). New York: Gryphon Editions.

James, W. (1961). *Psychology: The Briefer Course.* New York: Harper and Row.

Kant, I. (1989). *Foundations of the Metaphysics of Morals,* 2nd ed., trans. Beck, L. W. Pearson.

Kass, L. (2004). *Life, liberty and the Defense of Dignity: The Challenge for Bioethics.* San Francisco: Encounter Books.

Kateb, G. (2011). *Human Dignity.* Cambridge, Massachusetts: The Belknap Press of Harvard University Press.

Koehn, Daryl, and Leung, Alicia (2008). Dignity in Western versus in Chinese cultures: Overview and practical illustrations. *Business and Society Review, 113,* 4, 477–504.

Korman, A. (1968). Self-esteem, social influence and task performance: Some tests of a theory. *Proceeding of the 76th Psychoanalyst's Convention, 3,* 567–568.

Liu, D., and Baumeister, R. (2016). Social networking online and personality of self-worth: A meta-analysis. *Journal of Research in Personality, 64,* 79–89.

Macklin, R. (2003). Dignity is a useless concept. *British Medical* Journal, 237, 1419-20.

McCrudden, C. (2014). (Ed.). *Understanding Human Dignity.* London: Oxford University Press.

Marcel, G. (1963). *The Existential Background of Human Dignity.* Cambridge, Massachusetts: Harvard University Press.

Marsh, H. W., Parker, J. W., and Smith, I. D. (1982). Preadolescent self-concept: Its relation to self-concept inferred by teacher and to academic ability. *British Journal of Educational Psychology, 74,* 430–440.

Marsh, H. W., Relich, J. D., and Smith, I. D. (1983). Self-concept: The construct validity of interpretations based upon the SDQ. *Journal of Personality and Social Psychology, 45,* 6, 173–187.

Marsh, H. W., Smith, I. D., and Barnes, J. (1982). Multitrait-multimethod analyses of two self-concept instruments. *Journal of Educational Psychology, 74*, 430–440.

Marshall, S., Parker, P., Ciarrochi J., and Heaven, P. (2014). Is self-esteem cause or consequence of social support? A 4-year longitudinal study. *Child Development, 85, 3*, 1275–1291.

McCall, G. J., and J. L. Simmons (1966). *Identities and Interactions.* New York: Free Press.

Mead, G. H. (1934). *Mind, Self and Society.* Chicago: University of Chicago Press.

Mead, G. H. (1956). *The Social Psychology of George Herbert Mead* (A. Strauss, ed.). Chicago: University of Chicago Press.

Morsink, H. (1999). *Universal Declaration of Human Rights: Origins, Drafting and Intent.* Philadelphia: University of Pennsylvania Press.

Oxford English Dictionary (1970). London, England: Clarendon Press.

Pinker, Stephen (2008). The stupidity of dignity. *New Republic.* May 28.

Random House Dictionary of the English Language. (1973). New York: Random House.

Robins, R. W., and Trzesniewski, K. H. (2005). Self-esteem development across the lifespan. *Current Directions in Psychological Science, 14,* 3, 158–162.

Rosen, M. (2012). *Dignity: Its History and Meaning.* Cambridge, Massachusetts: Harvard University Press.

Rosenberg, M. (1979). *Conceiving the Self.* New York: Basic Books.

Sartre, J. P. (1948). *The Emotions: Outlines of a Theory.* New York: Philosophical Library.

Schopenhauer, A. (1965). *On the Basis of Morality.* Indianapolis: Hackett.

Shavelson, R. J., and Bolus, R. (1982). Self-concept: The interplay of theory and method. *Journal of Educational Psychology, 74,* 3–17.

Shavelson, R. J., Burnstein, L., and Keesling, J. W. (1977). Methodological considerations in interpreting research on self-concept. *Journal of Youth and Adolescence, 14,* 83–97.

Shavelson, R. J., Hubner, J. J., and Stanton, J. C. (1976). Self-concept: Validation of construct interpretations. *Review of Educational Research, 46*, 407–441.

Shavelson, R. J., and Stuart, K. R. (1981). "Application of causal modeling to the validation of self-concept interpretations of test scores." In Lynch, Gergen, and Norem-Hebelson (Eds.), *Self-Concept: Advances in Theory and Research.* Boston: Ballinger Press.

Shibutani, T. (1961). *Society and Personality.* Englewood Cliffs, NJ: Prentice-Hall.

Stern, A. (1975). On value and human dignity. *Listening,* 10, 74-90.

Stryker, S. (1968). Identity salience and role performance. *Journal of Marriage and the Family,* 4, 558-64.

Symonds, P. M. (1951). *The Ego and the Self.* New York: Appleton-Century Crofts.

Taylor, D. (1955). Changes in the self-concept without psychotherapy. *Journal of Consulting Psychology, 19,* 210–212.

Thibaut, J. W., and Kelley, H. H. (1959). *The Social Psychology of Groups.* New York: John Wiley and Sons.

Tunstall, W. W. (1985). *Dignity: A Psychological Construct.* Dissertations Abstracts International.

UNESCO Universal Declaration on Bioethics and Human Rights (2005). Malden, Massachusetts: Blackwell Publishing.

Van Maanen, J. (1979). "On the understanding of interpersonal relations." In W. Bennis, J. Van Maanen, E. H. Schein, and F. I. Steel, *Essays in Interpersonal Dynamics,* 13–42. Homewood, Illinois: Dorsey Press.

Waldron, Jeremy, with Wai Chee Dimock, Don Herzog, and Michael Rosen, edited by Meir Dan-Cohen (2015). *Dignity, Rank, and Rights.* The Berkley Tanner Lectures. Oxford University Press.

Wallis C, trans. 1995. *Revolution of Heavenly Spheres.* Amherst: Prometheus Books.

Webb, W. (1955). Self-evaluations, group evaluations and objective methods. *Journal of Consulting Psychology, 19,* 205–209.

Webster's New Twentieth Century Dictionary of the English Language Unabridged (1971). New York: The World Publishing Co.

Wells, L. E., and Marwell, G. (1976). *Self-Esteem: Its Conceptualization and Measurement.* Beverly Hills, California: Sage Publications.

Wouters, S., Doumen, S., Germeijs, V., Colpin, H., and Verschueren, K. (2013). Contingencies of self-worth in early adolescence: The antecedent role of perceived parenting. *Social Development, 22*, 2, 242–258.

Wylie, R. (1961). *The Self-Concept (Vol. 1).* Lincoln: University of Nebraska Press.

Wylie, R. C. (1979). *The Self-Concept (Vol. 2). Theory and Research on Selected Topics.* Lincoln: University of Nebraska Press.

Acknowledgments

It is with gratitude that I would like to acknowledge the contributions of:

Wolfgang O. von der Gruen, PhD and Patricia Sowards, PhD for their critical reading and constructive feedback of this book.

Additional appreciation is gratefully given for the support and guidance provided by my doctoral dissertation committee: Donelson R. Forsyth, PhD, committee chairman; Thomas H. Leahey, PhD; John M. Mahoney, PhD; Steven R. Robbins, PhD and James E. Lindsay, PhD

Index

A

A Common Area of
     Confusion 22
age 51
animal companions 60
Antle 32
apperception 27, 29
authenticity 26, 27

B

Bandura 30
Bandura's 30
Barnes 23
Baumeister 22, 71, 74, 76
Beane 15, 34
Beane & Lipka 15, 34
Bean & Lipka 23
being 59

belittling 47, 64
Berger 13
Berger & Luckman 13
bioethics xii
Blackhart 15
Bolus 31
Brownfiain 23
Burk 41, 42, 43, 44
Burke 44
Burns 22, 72
Burwell 24
busywork 35

C

Cahill 32
care giving 66
Chang 5, 72
Charles Darwin 62
Ciarrochi 23

clinical group 55, 56

clinical sample 55

co-create 25

collectivistic culture 53

conformation 19

Confucius 5

Cooley 13, 14, 72

Coopersmith 15, 23, 73

Copernicus 62

Crandal 22

Crocker 32

curvilinear relationship 51

D

Darwin 62

David Hume xiv

death with dignity 67, 68

decorative conception 11, 20

demeaning 47, 64

developmental disabilities ix, 66

Diggory 22, 73

dignified 19, 64

DIGNITAS 2

dignity ix, x, xi, xii, xiii, xiv, xv,
    xvi, xvii, 1, 2, 3, 4, 5, 6, 7, 8,
    9, 10, 11, 12, 15, 17, 18, 19,
    20, 21, 22, 23, 24, 25, 27, 28,
29, 30, 31, 33, 35, 36, 38, 39,
    40, 41, 42, 44, 45, 46, 48,
    49, 50, 51, 52, 53, 54, 55, 56,
    57, 58, 59, 60, 61, 63, 64, 65,
    66, 68, 76

Dignity and Bioethics 7

DIGNITY AND BIOETHICS 7

Dignity and Business 8

dignity and gender 50

Dignity and Human Rights 6

dignity and race 51

Dignity: A Psychological
    Construct ix

Dignity as Psychological
    Process 17

dignity as worth 19

Dignity is a Social Process 19

dignity's xii, xiv, xvi, 2, 10, 11, 17,
    18, 19, 24, 50, 56, 68

Ditzfeld 22

Dobson 15, 73

E

emergent 40

emergent phenomenon xii, 25,
    40, 46, 65

Emmanuel Kant 3

Erol 24

Erol & Orth 24

Evolving Meanings and Usage 1

F

Felix 32

Fitts 23

Fleming 15, 31

Fleming & Watts 15, 31

Foote 44

Forsyth 15

Foundations of the Metaphysics
of Morals 3

G

Gadin 24

Gadin & Hammarstrom 24

Galileo 62

Galileo Galilei 62

gender 50

Gergen 23

Giovanni Pico Della Mirandola 3

God 2, 4, 25

Gordon 23

Goudy 73

H

Hammarstrom 24

Harter 23

Harter, Waters & Whitesell 23

Heaven 24, 77

Homans' 38, 39

Hubner 31

human dignity 65

I

Immanuel Kant xv

incarcerate 30

individualistic culture 53

individualistic cultures 53

Interactionist Theory 40

interdependent 5, 13, 19, 25, 41,
54, 56, 57, 63, 66, 68

interpersonal exchanges 47

intersubjective 18

intersubjective psychological process 18, 21

invalidate 38, 41, 45, 47

invalidation 57

Invalidation 27

J

James 13, 14, 75
Jen 5
justification 19

K

Kant xv, 3, 75
Kass xiv
Kateb xiii, xiv, 75
Kelly 39
Knight 32
Korman 23

L

Language and Current Usage 9
law xii
Li 5
Lipka 15, 34
Liu 15
looking glass self 14
Luckman 13

M

Macklin xi

Macklin (2003) xi
Marcel 11, 20, 76
Marsh 15, 23
Marshall 23
Marshall et al 23
Marsh, Parker & Smith 23
Marsh, Relich & Smith 23
Marsh & Smith 15
Marsh, Smith & Barnes 23
Marwell 15, 22
McCall 42
McCall and Simmons 42
McCrudden xiii, xiv
McMahon 32
Mead 13, 14, 41, 77
meaning 10, 13, 25, 78
measurement requirements 42
medicine xii, 66
multidimensional model 23

N

Nagarajan 32
negative correlation 56
Nicolaus Copernicus 62
non-validation 20, 27, 28, 31, 35,
        46, 47, 48
nursing xii, 66

O

On the Origin of Species 62

ontology xvii, 59

Orth 24

P

paradoxical position 27

Parker 23

personal sense of worth 12, 15,
17, 18, 19, 21, 22, 23, 24, 26,
28, 29, 30, 31, 33, 34, 38, 39,
40, 41, 42, 45, 46, 48, 49,
54, 55, 61, 66

Personal Worth Inventory 37, 49

phenomenological ontology 19

phenomenology 20, 25, 26

philosophy xii

politics xii

positive correlation 58

power 11, 39, 48, 51

psychological 24

psychological process 24

PWI 37, 38, 49, 53, 54, 55, 56,
57, 58

R

race 51

ratification 19

reciprocal 56

reciprocal determinism 30

reflexive 13, 33, 34, 41, 43, 54

Relich 23

religion xii

Religious and Theological
Accounts 4

retirement 52

reward and punishment 38

Robins 24

Robins & Trzesniewski 24

Rosen xiii, xiv, 78, 80

Rosenberg 23, 31, 78

S

Sartre 13, 78

self-concept 15

self-conception 15, 22, 23, 24, 31,
33, 41

self-defeating 47, 57, 64

self-esteem 15, 22, 23, 32, 33, 34,
35, 36, 58, 64, 71, 72, 73,
74, 77, 78

self-images 44

self-structure 23, 31, 33, 46

self-worth 24

Shavelson 23, 31

Shavelson & Bolus 31

Shavelson, Hubner & Stanton 31

Shibutani 23

Showers 22

Simmons 42

Smith 15, 23

social interdependence 40

Stanton 23, 31

status 38

Stern, 25

St. Leo University ix

Stryker 43

suicide 48

symbolic interaction 25

Symonds 23

T

Taylor 23

the golden rule 64

The Latin Dignitas 2

theology xii

The Oxford English
    Dictionary 10

The Random House Unabridged
    Dictionary 10

The Reflexive nature of self-con-
    ception 13

Thibaut 39

Thibaut and Kelly 39, 80

Thomas Aquinas 2

Trzesniewski 24

U

United Nations Universal
    Declaration of Human
    Rights 6

university professors 37

V

validation 11, 19, 20, 21, 24, 25,
    26, 27, 28, 29, 30, 31, 33, 35,
    36, 37, 39, 40, 42, 43, 44, 45,
    46, 48, 58, 59, 60, 61, 63, 64,
    66, 67, 68, 69

valuation 20

Valuation 11, 20, 29

value 21

valuetive dimension 21

Van Mannen 14

Virginia Commonwealth
University xvi, 49, 55, 72,
75, 76, 77, 78, 80, 81
Vohs 22

W

Waldron xiii, xiv, 80
Waters 23
Watts 15, 31
weather 62
Webb 23
Webster's Unabridged
Dictionary 10
Wells 15, 22
Wells & Marwell 15, 22
Whitesell 23

work 52
worth 61
Worth/dignity 25
Wouters 24, 32
Wylie 22, 81

Z

Zeigler-Hill 22

Made in the USA
Middletown, DE
02 August 2018